TYPEWRITER

Paul Hetherington

TYPEWRITER
AND MANUSCRIPT

Typewriter

1.

The shed's old typewriter looks like eloquence, though its clattery love letters have vanished (with the regularity of beating wings the to-and-fro of the carriage return obscured my palimpsests). I recollect cadences, and gaucheness adhering like an impress. Time has whited most of it, though I see a girl loitering in a hallway offering me her life. I guess she meant marriage, and I may have said 'yes'. My subsequent letter skewed and dived like a severed pinion.

2.

Promises dissolve like crystals in water, while your lime-green jelly remains uneaten in the fridge. The impression of lights on the nearby hill is illusory. The roadway winds towards the harbour mouth, where last year a ferry churned and stalled, your scarf's chequered fabric diving and swimming. I turn back to bed as a snail's silver crawls along your shoulder, and walk outside under insistent fingers of rain. I'd mesh them in my fingers; I would gather them again.

3.

This isn't memory with its illusory pictures; nor is it something broken in the hand—a bird, perhaps, that flew into a window. The quality of feeling taints a friend's words—they couldn't have spoken better, and yet …. We're on a wooden deck, its boards bounce and a key drops into an overgrown yard. A year later you say, "I have it," holding up a piece of tarnished brass. But the lock it opened has been replaced and the conversation we were having when it fell … neither of us remembers the important words.

4.

Eventually darkness will lift from his eyes—even in day, it lies on his lids like grime. The story he started years ago will find its form, language like moths will launch from his tongue. If darkness has colonised his breathing, at last he'll breathe deeply again. He remembers a windowed view—a 'place carpeted with crimson'. That day his voice had sounded like a stranger's; another's accents usurped his own.

5.

He found the shore parsing its parts like a languorous sentence and stayed—although intending to return. Night was a black expostulation that he cowered beneath. But it grew familiar; the intractability of days became a relief. Driftwood and old sheets of iron made a home. Jellyfish washed up so often they were part of belonging. He found himself addressing the stars, realising his absurdity. Years gathered in his body like stores of salt; his voice was the sound of breakers.

6.

In the park, an old woman on a bench murmurs about what she's dropped—an earring that belonged to her mother. A bird perches for a moment on her shoulder, looking like a redbreast. He opens an envelope he's carried for three years and unfolds and straightens pages. Blue ink, a faint smell of oak or heather, a looping scrawl. Even after months the words are heavy—as if curlicues of metal; ideas that fret.

7.

In his family there was scant knowledge of others. A solitariness of long years lengthened through his mother's hands—an arm's reach of her grandmother's drowning (there, in her familiar English place, evading followers under a canal's mustard-yellow surface). His father's goodwill courted conversation, having left his mates from the war, de-mobbed into the middle classes. Drowning in his parents' reasonableness, he wanted a hand to lead him elsewhere. He bound himself to acts of language, cruelled by a sense of the abject, wandering into marshland with a girl who clambered over his tightening body. He made packets of words and thought 'this is a road away', listening for lament inside ordinary speech.

8.

When, after silence, small words returned, we tasted them eagerly. At first firm on the tongue, later they softened, fluttered and were small, pale moths that circled the cabbages—brushing cheeks, landing on arms. Night was woven with broken sentences. “Feel the air,” you said. Even our wine was saturated with words, and olives we placed in our mouths. Next morning we remembered the spillage—here and there, a red or blue word lay on the carpet. Our tongues felt the abrasions of speech. “What,” you asked, “have we said?”

9.

A woman in a crowd shouted as a train's whistle filled our ears. We failed to pay attention to a quietly-spoken boy. A cousin began a statement about family but an uncle intervened. And on a ferry we stared avidly, ignoring a phone call, marvelling at ancient trees and a radiant waterway. Some words we have tried without knowing how others speak.

10.

Sometimes your thoughts are ghostly and your utterances are not your own. Someone is standing in your body, speaking with your intonations. He wears his mask closely and has adopted your gestures. His words are cast in the colour of your skin. And when you manage to step into your name, your speaking includes him—but he's neither your doppelgänger nor your twin.

11.

He regathers yesterday's footsteps, walking past hedgerows and abandoned fields, taking the crumpled letter from his overcoat pocket and flattening its creases. The sun examines his hands, birds shrill and twitter. Her words are more obdurate than yesterday and still he fails to digest them. He begins to think of language as a difficult ascent—but gives the metaphor away.

12.

When I was a child I might have been a poor man's Alice, clambering under floorboards in old houses and imagining myself walking through mirrors. I drank dew with bugs and caterpillars; made greenest tea from miscellaneous leaves. I was neither girl nor boy, saying, "I am" to quell a sense of vanishing. The red queen came to lop off my head; I ducked, and swam in a spider web. I shrank to the size of a postage stamp as a mouse told me its implausible secrets.

13.

Rock pools rose and fell like atrial fibrillations, crabs stood under stone ceilings, words slid on sea-hammered ledges. I sat near them after escaping my parents' talk, listening to the waves' curdling murmur—words followed, parsing the sea's improbable syntax. I imagined myself an Ahab of the rocky shore, yet I tiptoed out, finding the rips' frayed edges.

14.

Space was not the stars' prickly gaze, or the long football field where I revelled. It was the scooping journey through self, as if a Milky Way was buried out of sight there. I trawled for patches of light, dragging the long darkness. For years, it was wading with an occluded moon. For decades it was picking at luminous patches, trying to find words. Prawns jumped and splashed, I stood in the sea's small corner and strangely knew it as being. That scarred face, the lost galaxies, the flying apart of thought.

15.

In the act of leaving she paused for minutes, dawdling at the entrance to the café. She'd sat there many days, with coffee and the view to the hills. It had been all promise: new colleagues, a slew of opportunities. Now she couldn't see it whole: tarnish on the doors; clogged words; a dropped fountain pen. She felt a tug, like promise's afterthought.

16.

An avenue of lindens pointed towards low hills and a bus with schoolchildren navigated pale dust. The woman next door brought a trussed hen and a basket of eggs, shyly murmuring. We studied maps and you said of your great aunt, as if commenting on topography: "I still see her crouching in the corners of rooms." Our words chased previous decades—a well where your rope-burnt grasp hauled water; an itinerant preacher relishing the lineaments of sin. We pegged washing as the schoolchildren returned screaming a ribald song, pointing and jeering. In the evening we reached for a cautious absolution; affection suited to raw and tender hands.

17.

Once again, much-rehearsed words balloon, carrying unexpected cargo. Night wind bangs shutters; we don't belong in the day. The room holds a width of conversation that resonates like a squally violin. It's time for Midnight Mass—you stand to see the church's familiar lights and people filing in. Why does the past behave like a preacher of the Apocrypha? Why does organ music sound like early snow?

18.

Trellises are covered in red roses and there's a sun as pale as an udder. Your words are like labial petals and I might be dressed in language, inhaling the flowers' scent. An old wall ambles next to us, stone after stone, and a cottage leans into three hundred years. You intimate what I've failed to know for decades. What we understand is not what we understood.

19.

Dalliances of light pull and shift, a landscape dissolves behind your elongated form, our romance is like syrup pooling at your feet. You become the shape of desire blown through by wind. Words we exchanged are as stiff as March flies and petals we fingered are charred. Time's a clock that neither of us reads.

20.

This is a monstrous possum settling into branches, a ceaseless breeze and night gathering memory's slow impostures. It's a house with rotten stumps and thousands of termites crawling; a disquisition on knowledge's impossibility. Fell the tree and the possum moves into the house, close windows and doors and the breeze hammers walls; replace stumps and still the house slides. The termites are carting pallid words; their explication drones like the wind; a voice says there's no time that this will not occur. Poems are debris that wind flusters.

21.

The clock bristles; walls are torrents on granite. Air hauls its updraughts; shore and sea collide on a shingle; words hoist strange inflections. There are rites of belonging—a sheep with cut throat and spilled entrails; a boy penned behind stakes; butter glistening in a bog. Dancing flares through the night with a wailing of ancient song. Clock hands are lifted pikes. What we speak we do not hear; what we claim we cannot possess.

22.

Just minutes ago she stuttered on the phone and Venice was muffled traffic noise. There was silence, as if unsaid words lay equalised—'teaspoon', 'love', 'doily', 'adventure', 'memory'. The large nouns had shrunk, banalities puffed out faces. Ten years, a shared wordhoard; now an archaic sound. The delicate parts of speech were drowned. In the watery world a monster walked.

23.

He began to read her as if he knew the text, offering analysis even as they were draped by sunrise. When she spoke of their pasts he failed to recognise himself. She busied herself, imagining him as an Egyptian mummy, wondering in what jar she'd find his heart. So many stones cut and carried with insolence; so much building of a sun-staring life, words like angular hieroglyphs. What lever could shift the weight of them?

24.

This language is the guttural wind and we're listening hard, as if it might be speaking the Atlantic's hidden history. So much turmoil, catching boulders with wayward threads. The world is stitched into one blanket as the storm utters its mysteries. It pours into the sea; it writes profusely on the sky's incandescent wax.

25.

With trowels and digital scans they reconstitute a world—dining areas, servants' quarters, bath houses, fortifications. A ceremonial axe, a ritual stone bowl, a broken crown's copper and gold. And a terse language of epithets and numbers, accounting for grain and burials. One room reveals frescoes of birds and gardens. We walk among them, imagining ourselves three thousand years younger, garnering ancient decision and feeling. You ask if it would be tolerable.

26.

Cursive experience lifts within the body—tissues of connection that pull as if the forty-year-old wound is fresh. No genre contains so many ellipses or stop-start narratives—and words that were beautifully said are incised as with a scalpel. Pink oleander flowers are impressed there, and shade like a printmaker's sudden black daub. Leave it alone, a psychologist insists, but it's spilling everywhere. New language tastes of it, and the drink that swills in the mouth.

27.

The letter is written on a single leaf, pressed into a book. Twenty years ago, on a loggers' rutted track, he'd stopped to help a stranger with a boiling radiator. Ten years ago that man had travelled half way round the world for his birthday; four years ago he'd nearly died repairing a snow-damaged roof. He'd always talked about "going into wilderness" and the note says nothing more will be spoken. Decades collapse into seven words.

28.

Stars again tonight and the old pain under the ribs. The river glitters with neglected promises. Her hands say 'silence', held to my shoulders by the moon's glue. We have much to discuss. Watching a bird rising over the river, we see into our futures.

29.

Sometimes when you wake, morning's first light is an invigilation. Your failures reach through a gap in the blind. In your mind's eye there's a long beach and sand creaks under your toes like an old settee. You find a song on your lips as the wind dissolves it. A figure swims towards you like an ungainly mermaid. Sea gathers you in an arm's sweep, and a gull's expostulation.

30.

He wakes to hear soft morning's raucous life running through the streets like an announcement. The city's aromas tumble in the room. Months ago, her absence faced him down in the eighth-floor bedroom; turning away, he chased the district's ancient gardens. In a nearby window a woman sprays perfume and the plants he kept alive through heat-waved summer have grown too heavy for the terrace. Tomorrow he will leave; his suitcase clasps a few tucked souvenirs.

31.

She held herself in light, near the window's rectangle. 'I belong; I don't belong,' she thought, knowing his words would be: 'Let me kiss you.' She could not, of course, as they bought coffee on the concourse. Angled light shifted, she stepped forwards and saw the near building's wall—red brick and scrolled ironwork. Beyond it, an ocean, like a painter's gesture, a view of white-topped waves. The swell arrived, as if she swam and was dragged under.

32.

"Well then," she said, picking up the tin, stirring the paint with a torn branch. He thought of the moon she'd depicted on rectangular canvas; how it gripped a tree fast in alien light; how a couple stood in red intimacy. He remembered their agreement—that he'd maintain the sprawling old place. When they'd arrived the guttering had sagged like a verbless sentence, and the deck was full of woodworm. He'd stripped off friable boards wondering what else was undermined. Now he dipped a brush, starting the colourful strokes.

33.

Flavours are words we speak—expressions as purple as lustrous aubergine; orange adjectives like the sweet potato; verbs as green as unripe fruit. You taste them again, saying, "This is most of what we have," dicing a cauliflower, making peppery hummus in a bowl. The horizon is the colour of caramelised sugar. You say, "Let's walk in the mouth of evening."

34.

A boy watches the steam train's chimney sparks, veering left on wind. The smell is of axle grease and combustion, above sedges and waterways where insects climb straws of light. There's a stick-bug with bright wings that he imagines as Icarus, and a dark fly like a heavy word, droning through gloom. It might be something he's yet to know; or a failed verb. A firefly dabbles at evening's edge.

35.

In rafters, an owl; in an outhouse, a young woman with hands on hips; at midnight, a pebble striking a window. Morning is compelled by words—stepping into a flow of syntax, claiming stubborn nouns, stumbling against adjectival colour, finding adverbial pleasure and prepositional intimations. A saddled horse whinnies; someone coughs in the yard.

36.

Eyes hold the strangest rooms. She is nearly fifteen, in a green tutu, making a pirouette à la quatrième derrière. The attic window's as grubby as her knees; when she falls forwards she's a dropping curtain. She holds his arms, laughing. She pulls her diary from a shelf. It says she doesn't love him; that he's much too young, and she points to where she's underscored the words. They kiss listlessly, and she's gone downstairs into the garden—a verb with sharp insect life.

37.

The school bell rings with the clatter of a child's chafing tugs. The ringers' roster is confined to a few favoured students—responsible citizens in a shoving world, where we parse sentences and gather collective nouns; where there's a bristle of milk bottles, soundings of teachers and a busy typewriter under a secretary's white hands. We arrive at school with a repartee that will fail.

38.

As if air opened a gap, or a hidden wound reddened night. My parents' voices continued with their reasonable sound, children laughed in the yard, pine needles rotted in shadow. I caught the breeze in my mouth, tasted clotted nouns. What was language saying?

39.

Memories stream like noise. A heavy tune rebounds from a dresser, climbing back into a radio. A girl stands in a primary school classroom reciting proper nouns—again he wonders at the failure of names. The effusions of a preacher rebound in a hall—something about grace; something about the cost of belief. A juggler holds up balls that might be shrunken heads. In the war he saw them nodding on a pole. Now, a nurse's irreverent, stray hand.

40.

Between long squalls and brief patterns of sunshine, catching his own breathing every few minutes, he still thinks of love—improbable, difficult fabric of belief. He finds himself daydreaming; sees himself in Venice buying gelato. The acqua alta runs over his boots as he stands in Piazza San Marco, imagining fifteenth century grandeur. Lines of poetry tighten his fingers, words net shoals of thought: he's young and running dune lines with a friend. He feels for his own hand and a notion of an ending.

Manuscript

1.

They'd shut the room because of structural problems. The ceiling leaned like inquiry; walls bulged with listless damp. You had a secret way there; a passage through crawling dark—a "priest's-hole kind of way" on hands and knees. I followed; we prised open chests and manuscripts, quizzing a mid-twentieth-century life—paid bills, love letters to a wife, out-of-date maps, brief notes about meetings with Amy-Jane—and you pressed against me, pointing towards parkland: "He must have loved the view," lying down among the papers. We never went back.

2.

So much writing; so many hours. But the bin's empty and the manuscripts are gone, the way a migraine eradicates thought. Courting meaning again and failing to find it—where are apposite words? Say it like this: a dance in limbs that a long dress hides; expressive concealments.

3.

He crawled in tunnels under earth. The periscopes he made reached into treetops and he watched the birds. Their scurry and fluster was entrancing; he adored the expansive mime of their song—breasts plumped; beaks thin trumpets. He examined his pasty skin and its sores, dusted his manuscript, wondering if sunlight would become him, after all. Might he also declaim?

4.

You believe you've seen that line of trees before. It is absence that's writing itself, that your body belonged to. Yet what was the colour of the house in the hills? Who snatched a toy from your hands? Hold a fork and knife as you learnt to do; pick up a novel you read at eight years old; see yourself near a fountain with new white skin—distances barely close even as thick drops fall on your face. You push a fork suddenly into your sister's arm.

5.

“Anyway,” she said, “after all our talk … .” We were still at odds but nodded agreement. It was the torn fabric we most regretted, hanging like rags. Words were pictures on that silk, but in just one evening … . Despite their price, you said they were “certainly” copies—but the man who’d sold them would have wept. What was damaged could be stitched, but wouldn’t be whole in the old way when, hand in hand, we took the long path down the hillside and ducked into a market stall. A young, black-haired woman gestured towards a curtain and the man slowly lifted those fragile silks from a drawer—obscure maps of the future.

6.

The distances between stars are small compared to airy hemispheres that separate us, words failing to make a bridge, daily doings unable to fortify the dark reduction. Remnant thought and feeling trundle through each week. Before I left you shifted food about a plate, bitten by pain. There was a day in November when I drafted your obituary and you visited me in a restaurant in Rome—I could barely believe you'd travelled that depth of sky. Later, looking at your final manuscripts, so many pages obscured your old inflections.

Typewriter
by Paul Hetherington

Acknowledgement for poems previously published is made to the following journals and anthologies: *Cities: Ten Cities; Ten Poets; The Stony Thursday Book; TEXT; Tract: Prose Poems.*

First published 2020

POETRY

ISBN: 978-0-6487825-1-3

BOOK, TYPESETTING, AND LOGO DESIGN
Mountains Brown Press

PUBLISHER
Life Before Man

Gazebo Books
PO Box 375
Summer Hill
New South Wales 2130
Australia

gazebobooks.com.au

COVER IMAGE: *Pistol No. 2*, 2019, oil on canvas, 56 x 40.5 cm, © Phil Day

www.ingramcontent.com/pod-product-compliance
Lightning Source LLC
LaVergne TN
LVHW051014080826
845145LV00009B/2618

* 9 7 8 0 6 4 8 7 8 2 5 1 3 *